MW00880377

Conversation Starters

for

Ellen Marie Wiseman's

What She Left Behind

By dailyBooks

  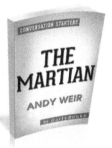

Tips for Using dailyBooks Conversation Starters:

EVERY GOOD BOOK CONTAINS A WORLD FAR DEEPER THAN the surface of its pages. The characters and their world come alive through the words on the pages, yet the characters and its world still live on. Questions herein are designed to bring us beneath the surface of the page and invite us into the world that lives on. These questions can be used to:

- Foster a deeper understanding of the book
- Promote an atmosphere of discussion for groups
- Assist in the study of the book, either individually or corporately
- Explore unseen realms of the book as never seen before

About Us:

THROUGH YEARS OF EXPERIENCE AND FIELD EXPERTISE, from newspaper featured book clubs to local library chapters, *dailyBooks* can bring your book discussion to life. Host your book party as we discuss some of today's most widely read books.

Table of Contents

Introducing *What She Left Behind*

ISABELLE STONE HAS A CHECKERED PAST. WHEN SHE WAS four years old, her mother shot her father in cold blood. Her defense tried to plead insanity, but her plea was dismissed. She was put behind bars for life, and Isabelle was brought up by her grandmother. She died when Isabelle was ten years old, at which point the little girl entered the foster system. Now, seventeen years old and with three foster homes in her past, Isabelle finds herself with Peg and Harry, a couple who shower her with love and trust, making life easier for her.

Peg, being the curator of the local museum, involves her family in the Willard Project. When the Willard Asylum shut down in 1995, an employee found a number of suitcases in the attic, and Peg wanted to delve into the mysteries of the pasts of some of these people. At this point, Isabelle comes across a diary from Clara Cartwright, a detainee in the asylum. She reads the diary and becomes interested in the woman. When she reads that Clara had a child that was forcibly taken away from her, she is determined to find that child and give her the suitcase.

Having her child forcibly abducted was not the only thing that Clara suffered in her life. She was in love with a recent Italian immigrant, Bruno Moretti. Her parents opposed the match and fixed her up with someone from their circle without her consent. But Clara rebelled, and when she got into an argument with her father, he called the doctor and had her committed to a posh asylum. She was imprisoned there against her will but was treated reasonably well.

When her father lost his money in the stock market crash, Clara's real nightmare started. She was sent off to Willard Asylum, a place with filthy bed linens, lack of bathroom infrastructure, and a basic lack of humanity. Clara tries to tell Dr. Roach about Bruno, but he brushes her off and tells her that Bruno never existed. When she finally gave birth, Roach steals her child, which he brings up as his own. When Bruno finally shows up to claim her, Roach has him committed against his will as well. The couple hatches an escape plan, during which Bruno is killed by the hospital staff. Clara is left to fend for herself and live out her life as a sane person in a mental asylum, being treated worse than a prisoner. She was a prisoner from 1929 to 1995, all because she spoke out for love.

Another thread running through the book is Isabelle's problems in high school with Shannon, the school bully. Her romance with Ethan and friendship with Alex helps her to deal with Shannon, and she discovers that Shannon too is a victim of child sexual abuse and neglect. Isabelle also finally discovers why her mother shot her father – he had been abusing her sexually. The differences in how society deals with problems is stark between then and now, but in some cases, the more things change, the more they remain the same.

Introducing the Author

AN AMERICAN WOMAN BASED IN NEW YORK, ELLEN MARIE Wiseman spent her childhood in Three Mile Bay, a small hamlet in New York. A first generation American with German roots, Wiseman frequently travels to Germany to visit her family. Her first book, *The Plum Tree*, published in 2013, was based on the experiences of her German mother. It was set during World War II and featured a woman trying to save her boyfriend, a Jewish man. It was very well received, and Wiseman has since written two more books, *What She Left Behind* and *Coal River*. She tends to write books that carry a strong sense of horror, inspired by real historical events. As a long-time lover of Stephen King, Anne Rice, and Dean Koontz, Wiseman had always expected to write something in the genre of horror or paranormal but has settled for historical horror instead.

Wiseman worked as a bookkeeper and did not have any formal education beyond high school. She had never even taken a creative writing course. She also did not have the benefit of a local writers' group. So when she determined to pursue her love of writing, she had to start from scratch. She turned to the Internet for help, and her search for a teacher led her to William

Kowalski, a Canadian novelist and screenwriter. The two hit it off, and Kowalski began to help Wiseman with her dream. He proved to be a good mentor and teacher and guided her through the challenge of learning how to be a storyteller.

Today, Wiseman lives on the shores of Lake Ontario with her husband and three dogs, two Shih Tzus and one Labrador. She also has two children, married and living with their own families. Her hobbies include reading, cooking, gardening, and traveling. She has written three books and is currently working on a fourth one.

Discussion Questions

. . . .

question 1

At the end, Nurse Trent claims that people didn't know any better then, so they tried horrific treatments on mental patients. Do you agree with this? Do you think this also covers the mistreatment of patients, such as having them live in complete filth, being slapped around, and so on? Discuss.

. . . .

. . . .

question 2

The doctor is shown as unscrupulous, the nurses as blind to the sufferings of the patients, and the orderlies as violent. What kind of people do you think chose to work in a mental asylum? Do you think people became nasty when they started working there or were nasty people attracted to the work? Give reasons.

. . . .

. . . .

question 3

Of all the "treatments" mentioned in the book, which one do you think is the worst, and why?

. . . .

. . . .

question 4

New York State has sealed the records of these patients, ostensibly to
"protect their privacy." Do you think this is the real reason? Why do you
think this step has been taken? Do you think the descendants of these victims
have the right to know what happened to their long-forgotten ancestors?
Discuss.

. . . .

question 5

Isabelle keeps talking about mental illness being contagious. Do you think
this is a common misconception? How can mental health education be
improved?

. . . .

· ·

question 6

Clara was sent away by her father for refusing to marry the man her parents chose for her. She also blamed her father's harsh behavior for her brother's suicide. How far do you think Henry Cartwright was responsible for his son's death?

· ·

. . . .

question 7

Isabelle's mother refused to allow a physical examination of her after she was molested by her father. Why do you think Joyce refused to allow a medical checkup and preferred to go to prison instead?

. . . .

question 8

Clara is forcibly sterilized against her will or knowledge during her time at Willard. This was common practice in state asylums in the United States. How far do you think we have come today in allowing women to make reproductive decisions that would mostly affect them and their bodies?

. . . .

question 9

There are two voices in the story: Isabelle and Clara. Which one did you enjoy the most, and why? Which one did you relate to the most, and why?

question 10

Isabelle had lived in foster homes throughout her childhood since the age of ten. Peg and Harry were her fourth foster family. How do you think such constant changes affect children during their most important years?

question 11

Isabelle talks about the foster families where she felt unwelcome or neglected. Why do you think such people take in foster children? What can be done to help such children? Do you think foster children are ready to strike out on their own at the age of eighteen? What facilities do you think could benefit them once they are of age and phased out of the foster system?

. . . .

question 12

Shannon is a bully and goes to criminal extents to persecute Isabelle without any good reason. She is supported by the entire class, some supporting her actively while others are looking away when she is bullying someone. Do you find this realistic? Why do you think Shannon has such power over her classmates?

. . . .

. . . .

question 13

A large number of women were sent to Willard during its existence for extramarital affairs, disobeying the man of the family, postpartum depression, and not getting over the grief of losing a spouse within three months or so. Do you think the family members of these women ever thought about them? Did they think that the patients were being treated well or didn't they care?

. . . .

. . . .

question 14

Many people were admitted to the asylum for no reason, and some had very
manageable illnesses such as postpartum depression or epilepsy. How do you
think the condition of the asylum and the terrible treatments they had to
undergo affected them?

. . . .

. . . .

question 15

Clara's parents never looked back after sending their only daughter away. What do you think they did after her departure? Did they genuinely feel this was the right thing to do for Clara's sake? How do you think they reconciled to the loss of their two children?

. . . .

. . . .

question 16

Women's Fiction Writers featured a review in which it claimed that the two
story lines of Clara and Isabelle are interconnected in overt and subtle ways
throughout the novel. Can you list the ways in which the two stories are
interconnected? Discuss.

. . . .

. . . .

question 17

The review in *Women's Fiction Writers* claims that the complex journeys of its main characters, Clara and Izzy, makes the book women's fiction. Do you agree? What is your understanding of women's fiction? Is there a men's fiction genre too? What would this genre contain?

. . . .

. . . .

question 18

In its review, *Historical Novel Society* claims that Isabelle's story reads like a young adult novel at times. Do you agree? What aspects of the plot make it appear like a young adult novel?

. . . .

. . . .

question 19

The blog, *Psychiatry Talk*, published a review of the book in which it claims
that there were vivid descriptions of the treatment that was done at that time.
Do you agree? What have you learned about the treatments used in the past in
mental asylums?

. . . .

. . . .

question 20

In *Psychiatry Talk*, the reviewer expresses their opinion that it would not have been possible for someone to be committed to a mental institution merely on the word of her father if they did not have a mental illness. Do you agree? Can you find real historical cases of women being held against their will in mental asylums? Discuss.

. . . .

  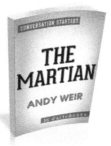

. . . .

question 21

The blog, *Reviews & More*, claims that the book reminds us that the human
need to belong to a family is as essential as air. Do you agree? What
important role does a family fulfill in our lives? What happens when the same
family betrays us?

. . . .

question 22

Miss Kirtley's Blog featured a review in which Isabella's story is claimed to be clichéd. Do you agree? What do you find clichéd about it? How do you think this story could have been improved? Discuss.

. . . .

question 23

Good Book Fairy compares *Blue Asylum* by Kathy Hepinstall to *What She Left Behind.* What are the similarities between these two books?

. . . .

· ·

question 24

In the blog *Anita Loves Books*, the reviewer says that the ease at which Clara's father was able to have her committed was frightening. What did you find the most frightening in the book, and why?

· ·

. . . .

question 25

Spa Week Daily published a review in which it states that the book portrays
that what it takes to know and understand oneself is to fully understand
somebody else. Do you agree with this? What other messages did the book
have?

. . . .

question 26

Wiseman had no formal education after high school or any experience or training in creative writing. She was mentored by another author, William Kowalski, who guided her through the learning process. What kind of background does one require to be a successful writer? Does having a degree help in getting a head start?

. . . .

question 27

Wiseman writes historical fiction but has chosen topics that showcase the
terrible aspects in our past. Why do you think she chooses these heavy
topics?

. . . .

· ·

question 28

When she wanted to begin writing, Wiseman turned to the internet for help and found a good mentor in the form of William Kowalski. How do you think the internet has changed the lives of writers today?

· ·

. . . .

question 29

Wiseman loves books by authors such as Stephen King, Anne Rice, and Dean Koontz. Can you find any similarities to these authors in her books? Discuss.

. . . .

. . . .

question 30

Wiseman has written three books so far. Which one of them would you like
to see adapted into a movie, and why?

. . . .

. . . .

question 31

Clara and Bruno came from very different backgrounds, both financially and culturally. If the path of love had been smooth, do you think they would have remained happily married? What does it take to make a multicultural, financially disparate marriage work?

. . . .

. . . .

question 32

Clara had refused to marry James and confronted her father about her brother's suicide. This was when he called the police and had her committed. If you were in Clara's place, what would you have done, and why?

. . . .

. . . .

question 33

Crystal, Ethan, Luke, and others from the school give in to Shannon's temper tantrums and always let her have her way. If you were in this group of friends, what would you have done when it came to playing cruel pranks on innocent people, and why?

. . . .

. . . .

question 34

Isabelle's mother shot her father when she discovered him trying to molest Isabelle. How would Isabelle's life have turned out if Joyce had taken the sensible way out and called in the police?

. . . .

. . . .

question 35

The nursing staff, orderlies, and even the doctors in the psychiatric hospital were hard-hearted and cruel. If you worked in a mental asylum in the 1930s, how would you have dealt with the way the patients were treated?

. . . .

. . . .

question 36

Clara is fully sane but is committed to a mental asylum because her father felt
threatened by her. If you were Clara, how do you think you would have
handled being in such a place all your life? Would you feel that meeting your
daughter at the end of your life is sufficient for a happy ending? Discuss.

. . . .

. . . .

question 37

Isabelle had a past of abandonment and neglect and being shunted from one foster home to another. What do you think would have happened to her if she had lived during Clara's time?

. . . .

question 38

Bruno was a poor first generation Italian immigrant. When he came to rescue Clara from Willard Asylum, he ended up being forcibly detained as well. He is also murdered in a bid to escape. How do you think things might have been different for Bruno, and consequently Clara, if Bruno had a rich and powerful family?

. . . .

Quiz Questions

. . . .

question 39

Clara's baby was adopted by _____.

. . . .

question 40

Clara and Bruno meet for the first time at _____.

. . . .

question 41

True or False: Dr. Roach tells Clara that Bruno is dead.

. . . .

. . . .

question 42

Clara was first sent to the _____.

. . . .

question 43

_____ gave Isabelle information about Clara.

question 44

_____ was the school bully who tried to terrorize Isabelle.

· ·

question 45

Peg and Harry were the _____ family to take in Isabelle under the foster system.

· ·

question 46

Wiseman's first published book was titled _____.

question 47

Wiseman grew up in _____.

question 48

_____ is Wiseman's mentor.

question 49

Wiseman has _____ roots.

question 50

Wiseman worked as a _____ before she became a writer.

Quiz Answers

1. Dr. Roach
2. Cotton Club
3. False; Roach tells Clara that Bruno does not exist and is a figment of her imagination.
4. Long Island Home
5. Nurse Trent
6. Shannon
7. Fourth
8. The Plum Tree
9. New York
10. William Kowalski
11. German
12. Bookkeeper

THE END

Want to promote your book group? Register here.

 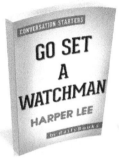 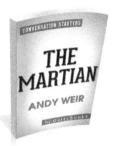

Made in United States
Orlando, FL
28 January 2022

14176026R00036